SCIENCE EXPERIMENTS WITH

LIGHT

A Division of ABDO

ABDO
Publishing Company

BY ALEX KUSKOWSKI   Consulting Editor, Diane Craig, M.A./Reading Specialist

visit us at www.abdopublishing.com

Published by ABDO Publishing Company, a division of ABDO, P.O. Box 398166, Minneapolis, Minnesota 55439. Copyright © 2014 by Abdo Consulting Group, Inc. International copyrights reserved in all countries. No part of this book may be reproduced in any form without written permission from the publisher. Super SandCastle™ is a trademark and logo of ABDO Publishing Company.

Printed in the United States of America, North Mankato, Minnesota
062013
112013

♻ PRINTED ON RECYCLED PAPER

Editor: Liz Salzmann
Content Developer: Alex Kuskowski
Cover and Interior Design and Production: Mighty Media, Inc.
Photo Credits: Aaron DeYoe, Shutterstock

The following manufacturers/names appearing in this book are trademarks: Duracell®, Fiskars®, Jell-O®, Learning Resources®, Maglite®, Pyrex®, Sanalac®, Sharpie®, Total®, Ping-Pong®

Library of Congress Cataloging-in-Publication Data
Kuskowski, Alex.
  Science Experiments with light / by Alex Kuskowski ; consulting editor, Diane Craig.
    p. cm. -- (More super simple science)
  Audience: 005-010.
  ISBN 978-1-61783-851-4
1. Light--Experiments--Juvenile literature. 2. Science--Methodology--Juvenile literature. I. Craig, Diane. II. Title.
  QC360.K87 2014
  535.078--dc23
                2012049830

Super SandCastle™ books are created by a team of professional educators, reading specialists, and content developers around five essential components—phonemic awareness, phonics, vocabulary, text comprehension, and fluency—to assist young readers as they develop reading skills and strategies and increase their general knowledge. All books are written, reviewed, and leveled for guided reading, early reading intervention, and Accelerated Reader® programs for use in shared, guided, and independent reading and writing activities to support a balanced approach to literacy instruction.

TO ADULT HELPERS

Learning about science is fun and simple to do. There are just a few things to remember to keep kids safe. Some activities in this book recommend adult supervision. Be sure to review the activities before starting, and be ready to assist your budding scientist when necessary.

KEY SYMBOLS

Look for these symbols in this book.

SHARP!
You will be working with a sharp object. Get help!

HOT!
You will be working with something hot. Get help!

TABLE OF CONTENTS

SUPER SIMPLE SCIENCE

You can be a scientist! It's super simple. Science is all around you. Learning about the world around you is part of the fun of science. Science is in your house, your backyard, and on the playground.

Find science in gelatin and water. Look for science with flashlights and lasers. Try the activities in this book. You'll never know where to find science unless you look!

SCIENCE WITH LIGHT

Use light to learn about science. Science explains how to light a lightbulb. Science shows you how to make light **bounce**! In this book you will see how light can help you learn about science.

WORK LIKE A SCIENTIST

Scientists have a special way of working. It is a series of steps called the Scientific Method. Follow the steps to work like a scientist.

1. Look at something. What do you see? What does it do?

2. Think of a question about the thing you are watching. What is it like? Why is it like that? How did it get that way?

3. Think of a possible answer to the question.

4. Do a test to find out if you are right. Write down what happened.

5. Think about it. Were you right? Why or why not?

KEEP TRACK

There's another way to be just like a scientist. Scientists make notes about everything they do. So get a notebook. When you do an experiment, write down what happens in each step. It's super simple!

WHAT YOU WILL NEED

2-liter plastic bottle

9 × 13-inch glass baking dish

30-60-90 triangle

aluminum foil

black paint, paintbrush, & foam brush

books

bowls

cardboard & cardboard box

cereal box

chenille stems

clay

compact disc

cookie cutters

D battery

dinner knife

drinking glass

drinking straws

flashlight & flashlight bulb

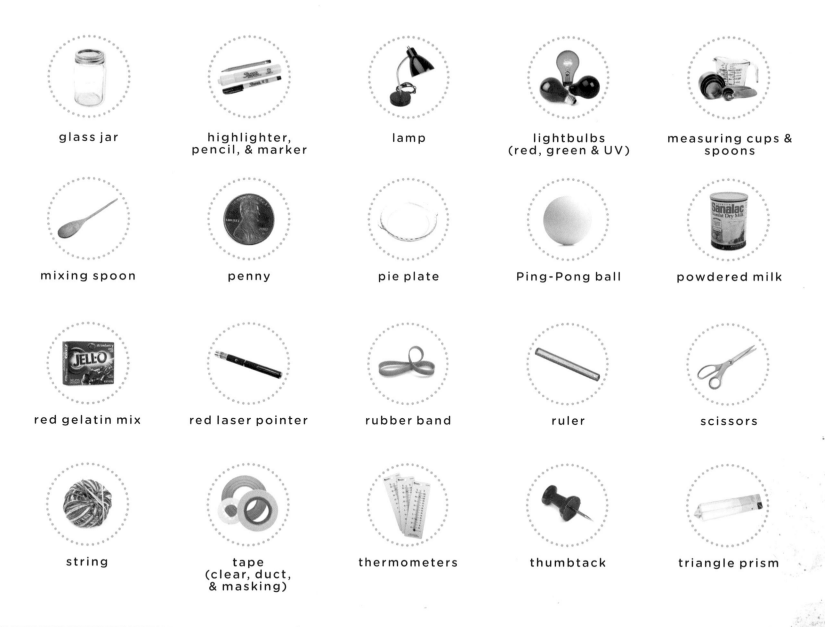

glass jar

highlighter,
pencil, & marker

lamp

lightbulbs
(red, green & UV)

measuring cups &
spoons

mixing spoon

penny

pie plate

Ping-Pong ball

powdered milk

red gelatin mix

red laser pointer

rubber band

ruler

scissors

string

tape
(clear, duct,
& masking)

thermometers

thumbtack

triangle prism

01 WATER & LIGHT WAVES

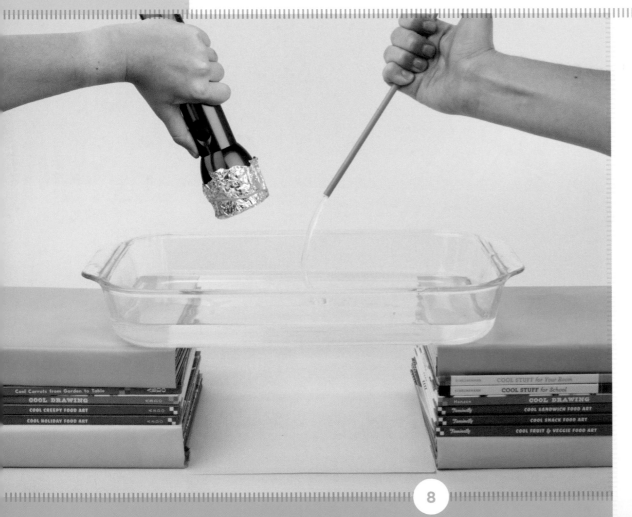

WHAT YOU WILL NEED

books

ruler

paper

9 × 13-inch glass baking dish

measuring cup

water

flashlight

aluminum foil

rubber band

pencil

drinking straw

DIRECTIONS

1. Make 2 even piles of books. They should be 4 inches (10 cm) high and 8½ inches (21 cm) apart. Put a sheet of paper between the piles. Set the dish on the books. Put 1 cup of water in it.

2. Cover the flashlight with foil. Wrap a rubber band around it. Poke a hole in the foil with a pencil.

3. Dip one end of the straw in the water. Cover the other end with your thumb.

4. Shine the flashlight on the dish. Lift the straw out of the water. Take your thumb off the end. Watch the paper under the dish.

WHAT'S GOING ON?

Light and water move in waves. The waves make shadows on the paper. They show how light moves. A darker shadow is the high part of a wave. A lighter shadow is the low part of a wave.

02 RADICAL LIGHT REFRACTION

WHAT YOU WILL NEED

- medium bowl
- penny
- clear tape
- water
- measuring cup
- clear drinking glass
- pencil

DIRECTIONS PART 1

1. Tape the penny inside the bowl.

2. Move back until the edge of the bowl hides the penny.

3. Keep your head still. Pour water slowly into the bowl until it is full. What do you see?

WHAT'S GOING ON?

Water causes light to bend. This is called **refraction**. At first, the edge of the bowl blocked the penny. Adding water refracted the light. It bent it enough for you to see the penny.

DIRECTIONS PART 2

④ Fill the glass at least halfway with water.

⑤ Put the pencil in the water. Hold the pencil straight up and down. Make sure it is touching the bottom.

6 Look at the pencil from the side. How does it look?

⑦ Let go of the pencil. Now look from the side again. What is different?

WHAT'S GOING ON?

The light **refracts** where the air and water meet. When the pencil is at an angle, it looks broken. The part in the water does not line up with the part out of the water.

EXPERIMENT

03 SUPER SIMPLE SPECTROMETER

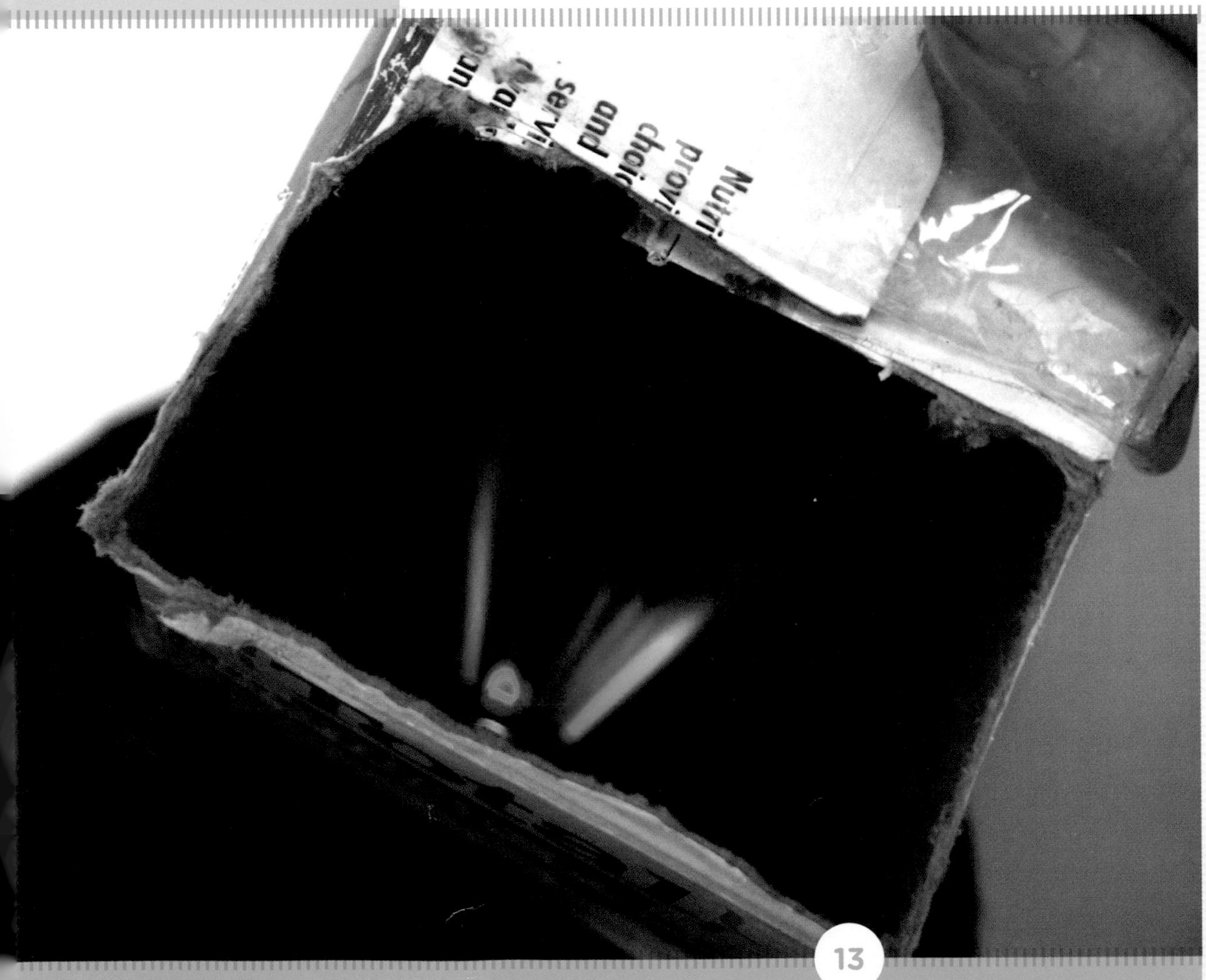

WHAT YOU WILL NEED

cereal box

ruler

scissors

marker

30-60-90 triangle

compact disc

duct tape

flashlight

DIRECTIONS

① On one side of the box, measure 4 inches (10 cm) down from the top. Draw a 1-inch (2.5 cm), **horizontal** line. Cut a very narrow **slit** along the line.

② On the top of the box, measure 1½ inches (4 cm) from the side opposite the slit. Make a mark. Cut off the box top from the mark to the side.

③ On the side opposite the slit, measure 4½ inches (11 cm) down from the top. Draw a line across the side to mark it.

④ Place the 30-60-90 triangle on the box. Line the short side up with the side of the box. The corner should be even with the line across the side. Draw a 2-inch (5 cm) line in from the edge. Repeat on the back. Cut along the three lines.

⑤ Slide the compact disc into the **slot** made by the cuts. The shiny side should face up. Push it in halfway.

⑥ Use duct tape to cover the slot and keep the compact disc in place.

7 Shine the light into the narrow **slit**. Look through the hole on the top of the box.

WHAT'S GOING ON?

Light is made up of many colors. When light hits the compact disc, it spreads out. You can see all of the colors. This is called a **spectrum**. A **spectrometer** shows all the colors in a light spectrum.

LASER LIGHT REFLECTION

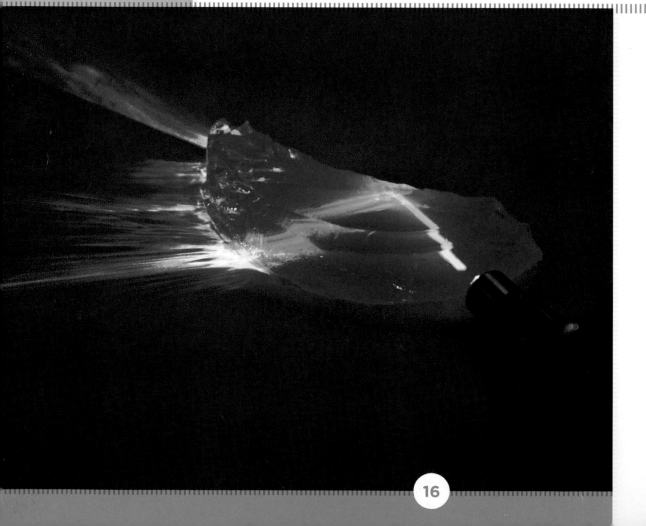

WHAT YOU WILL NEED

medium bowl

red gelatin mix

measuring cups

water

pie plate

dinner knife

cookie cutters

red laser pointer

DIRECTIONS

1. Make the gelatin in the pie plate. Have an adult help you follow the directions on the box.

2. Cut the gelatin into different shapes. Use a knife or cookie cutters.

3. Turn off the lights. Shine the laser through one of the gelatin shapes. Point it at an angle through one side. What happens?

4. Point the laser through the other shapes. Can you make the light **bounce** or bend?

WHAT'S GOING ON?

The inside walls of the gelatin reflect light. The reflection makes the light change direction. It bounces around inside the gelatin.

①

②

③

05 EERIE SHIFTING SHADOWS

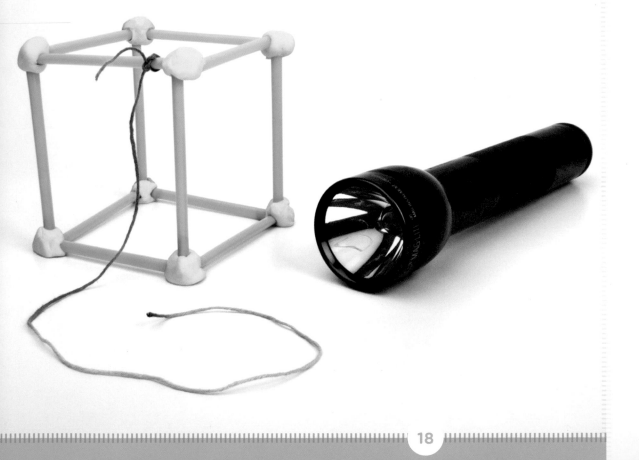

WHAT YOU WILL NEED

6 drinking straws

scissors

clay

ruler

6-inch (15 cm) string

paper

flashlight

DIRECTIONS

1. Cut the straws in half. Roll eight balls of clay. Make them 1 inch (2.5 cm) wide.

2. Use clay balls to connect four straw pieces into a square. Make a second square the same way.

3. Use the last four straw pieces to connect the two squares. This makes a cube.

4. Tie the string to one of the straws.

5. Prop up the paper. Pick up the cube by the string. Hold it in front of the paper. Point the flashlight at the cube. Spin the cube slowly. Watch the shadow on the paper.

WHAT'S GOING ON?

Your eyes see the cube going one direction. Your brain sees the shadow on the paper switching directions.

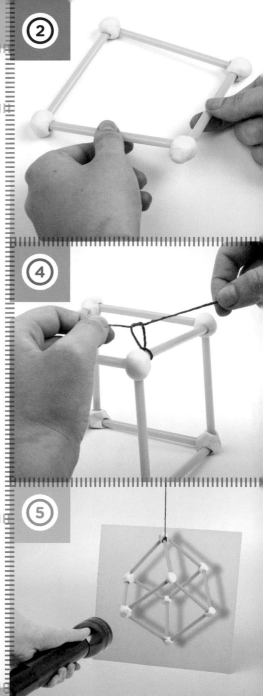

06 RED LIGHT, GREEN LIGHT

WHAT YOU WILL NEED

2 lamps

ruler

1 red lightbulb

1 green lightbulb

Ping-Pong ball

cardboard

DIRECTIONS

1. Set the lamps 1 foot (30 cm) apart. Put the Ping-Pong ball between them. Make sure it is the same distance from each lamp. Put the red bulb in one lamp. Put the green bulb in the other lamp.

2. Turn the lamps on. Turn off any other lights in the room. Hold the cardboard in front of the red lamp. Look at the ball.

3. Hold the cardboard in front of the green lamp. Look at the ball.

4. Set the cardboard aside. Look at the ball. What happens?

WHAT'S GOING ON?

The lights create different color shadows. If one light is blocked, the shadow is the color of the unblocked light. Both lights mix to make a yellow shadow.

07

BENDING LIGHT BEAMS

WHAT YOU WILL NEED

2-liter plastic bottle

black paint

foam brush

thumbtack

tape

water

9 × 13-inch glass baking dish

red laser pointer

DIRECTIONS

① Paint a large black square halfway around the bottle. Let the paint dry. Repeat until the black is solid.

② Poke a hole in the center of the square with the thumbtack. Place a piece of tape over the hole.

③ Fill the bottle with water. Put it in the baking dish. Shine the laser through the clear side of the bottle toward the hole.

4 Take off the tape. Turn off the lights. What happens? Try putting your hand in the stream of water. What happens?

WHAT'S GOING ON?

The light **bounces** inside of the stream of water. Some light escapes. It makes the stream glow. The light stays in the water until the water hits something.

(08) LIGHT UP THE WORLD

WHAT YOU WILL NEED

- aluminum foil
- scissors
- ruler
- tape
- 1 D battery
- 1 flashlight bulb

DIRECTIONS

1. Cut two strips of aluminum foil. Make them ¼ inch (.5 cm) by 6 inches (15 cm).

2. Tape one strip to the bottom of the battery. Tape one strip to the top of the battery.

3. Rest the bulb on the bottom strip of foil.

4. Touch the top strip to the metal side of the bulb.

WHAT'S GOING ON?

Aluminum is a metal. It carries an electric current between the battery and the bulb. The bulb lights up!

25

09 TOP SECRET GLOWING LIGHTS

WHAT YOU WILL NEED

UV lightbulb

lamp

clear drinking glass

water

highlighter

chenille stem

string

26

DIRECTIONS

1. Put the UV lightbulb in the lamp. Fill the glass with water. Shine the lamp on the water. Does anything happen?

2. Put the highlighter in the glass, marker tip down. Wait 1 hour.

3. Take the highlighter out. Turn off other lights. Shine the lamp on the water. What happens?

4. Put the chenille stem and the string in the glass. Wait 2 hours. Take the stem and string out. Let them dry. Shine the lamp on them. What happens?

WHAT'S GOING ON?

The UV lightbulb shines light that usually can't be seen by human eyes. The highlighter ink contains **phosphors**. The UV light makes the phosphors glow.

⑩ SUN BRIGHT, SKY LIGHT

WHAT YOU WILL NEED

glass jar

water

measuring spoons

½ teaspoon powdered milk

mixing spoon

flashlight

DIRECTIONS

① Fill the jar with water. Add the powdered milk. Stir well.

② Take the jar and flashlight into a dark room. Shine the flashlight at the liquid from above. What color is the milk?

③ Put the flashlight against the bottom the jar. What color is the surface of the milk?

WHAT'S GOING ON?

The crystals in the milk are like the Earth's atmosphere. Light shining from above is like light during the day. It looks blue. Light shining from below is like a sunset. It looks orange.

11 MEASURE A RAINBOW

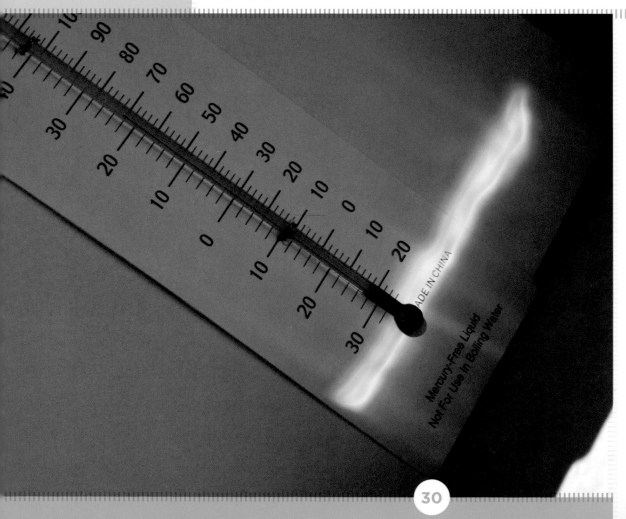

WHAT YOU WILL NEED

3 thermometers

white paper

paintbrush

black paint

triangle prism

cardboard box

masking tape

DIRECTIONS

1. Set the thermometers on paper. Write down the temperature. Paint the bulbs of the thermometers black. Let the paint dry.

2. Tape the prism inside the box along a top edge.

3. Put paper in the bottom of the box. Place the box so sunlight shines through the prism. Find the rainbow on the paper.

4. Put one thermometer in blue light. Put another in yellow light. Put the last thermometer just beyond the red light. Wait 10 minutes. Write down the new temperatures.

WHAT'S GOING ON?

Each color of light has a different temperature. The coolest is blue. The hottest is a type of light that you can't see. It's next to the red light. It's called infrared light.

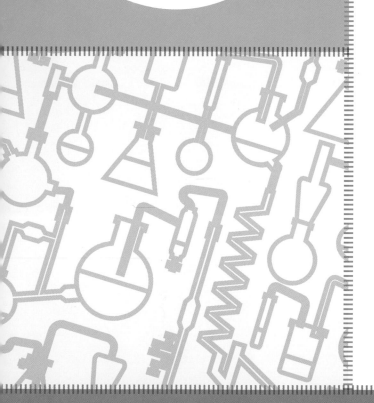

GLOSSARY

bounce – to spring up or back after hitting something.

horizontal – in the same direction as the ground, or side-to-side.

phosphor – something that gives off light after the light source is removed.

refract – to cause to a ray, such as light, to bend when it passes at an angle from one medium into another, such as from air into water.

slit – a narrow cut or opening.

slot – a narrow opening.

spectrometer – a tool for creating a spectrum.

spectrum – the range of colors revealed in light through a rainbow or prism.